Shelter under the Sun

Poetry of Three Hungarian Women

Borbála Kulin

Zita Izsó

Krisztina Rita Molnár

Translated by Gabor G Gyukics

The poets wish to acknowledge these publications:

Borbála Kulin https://www.unlikelystories.org/
 content/failure

Zita Izsó https://www.unlikelystories.org/content/a-long-time-
no-see-relative-and-as-the-offspring-of-the-cichlids

Krisztina Rita Molnár
https://www.unlikelystories.org/content/stare-the-cloud

The press expresses its appreciation to the Petofi Literary Fund
for a grant in support of the translation of the poems by Gabor G
Gyukics.

PETŐFI
LITERARY
FUND

Cover art by Sára Pozsgai

Library of Congress Control Number: 2021948763

Published by Singing Bone Press

Singingbonepress.com

ISBN: 978-0-933439-31-3

Table of Contents

Preface

Borbála Kulin

Where We Didn't Even Start

Borbála Kulin

Where We Didn't Even Start

Zita Izsó
Arrival

Krisztina Rita Molnár
Report

Preface

In the first half of the last century, there were serious debates in Hungarian literature about whether a woman could write professionally and, if so, what and how. Can anything a woman writes be worthy of attention or is what she has to say relevant on only certain well-defined topics?

The echoes of those debates haunt the poets in this volume, too. It would be difficult to ignore the fact that these poems were written by women, even though it is equally difficult to capture what their specifications are. The way they see the world, their visions and methods are different. Still they are united by a common point of view. From this perspective the world is alien, often hostile, incomprehensible, and operates according to rules that are not their own, and "I," the speaker, pays the price. Still it doesn't seem to be changeable within the framework of our long-standing social parlor game. The game itself is the problem, so the poems of this book constantly bump into the walls of the game, questioning it and revealing its absurdity—the absurdity that remains hidden from the players, forever.

Borbála Kulin's poetry is the closest to what—at least in Central European literature—has traditionally been expected of women poets in subject matter and approach. Her poems deal with love, home, the experience of the female body, individuality, and uniqueness. She tries to describe and make sense of a world that constantly confines and hurts even those who make every effort to adapt to it. But the image breaks into fractal-like, self-repeating pixels and the concepts of woman, mother, family, home, country, and body lose their meanings. The impossibility of being at home goes beyond the actual geographic and social reasons, but the speaker of the poems can still find her voice in the tiny, preserved pieces of this fragmented worldview.

In **Zita Izsó's** poems it is as if the speech situations of her poems illustrate the famous words of the internationally renowned psychologist András Feldmár on trauma: "Trauma in reality is not what happened to you, but the fact that it's impossible to talk about it to anyone. The experience is frozen." Izsó's poetry—using images of ice, melting, and freezing—renders this experience with incredible power. The self in the poems speaks for all the silenced, swept-under-the-carpet, "collateral" victims, and does so without dissolving their exclusion. The horror and inhumanity of what has happened to the victims strike our hearts because they use a language which they are excluded from. This language is so solid and safe because it makes certain things unspeakable and certain experiences taboos. When we see them, we look away and pretend nothing has happened. Izsó makes these experiences speak so we know we are dealing with people who blame themselves for what they went through. Domestic violence, terminal illness, traumas of war, the exclusion and vulnerability of homeless refugees are all addressed in these poems. In addition, poems treat the traditional, traumatic experiences of womanhood—infertility, giving birth to a disabled child, harassment, rape. Behind her images an alien meaning emerges, the language that talks about a world in which words could never be born. These are heavy, powerful poems of indispensable confrontation. They show that in the reality of experience there is no private and foreign, that the boundaries of the common and the personal are within us, and that they are mere illusions. This universal level of experience and empathy, which can be called Christlike, without exaggeration, makes her poems an authentic, unflinching voice of morality without becoming dogmatic, moralizing, or offering false comfort or absolution.

The speaker's language in **Krisztina Rita Molnár's** poetry circulates like an elusive, untraceable patch of light among the objects and occurrences of the world, society, and history: always flying to a new place, hiding its source and body from us. She doesn't call anything her own. She has no home, though she is able to reach and observe every place. She is playing, pointing out surprising moments to wonder at, but before being fully absorbed in it, she moves on. Yet her attention is like a child's, exquisite and straightforward. The poems point things out, raising them into conscious as their most important task. As the poem Oil Lamp conceives it (paraphrasing the biblical parable of the wise and foolish virgins with multiple irony), the goal is to maintain the boundary. But this is only an indication, a signal to the ever-moving line between conscious and unconscious. There is no need to do anything else. These poems suggest that this boundary, the moment of this glance and attention, are what we really are. So any kind of perpetuance and solidification would imprison the playful, ever-wandering, always-in-motion light of consciousness. That is why Krisztina Rita Molnár's poetry keeps the reader in perpetual motion. If we would feel that we understand, she immediately marks it, makes the situation uncertain by the conscious, reflective use of form, rhythm, and rhyme. The poem's speaker gives us an ironic wry look and disappears. In the Persian rug in her poem "A Million Stitches" readers can see both sides of it. We won't step on it with the certainty that it's ours, as it's "rightfully ours", and we are at home with it.

Orsolya Rákai, literary scholar and
Associate Professor of the University of Szeged

BORBÁLA KULIN

WHERE WE DIDN'T EVEN START

Where We Didn't Even Start ≈ Ahol el se kezdtük

It hurts that you can't really love me.
I am coming to see you, in vain. You
dissuade me from yourself
with your every motion.
There are jumbled worlds
on the unfolded couch.
I've believed we could crumple the
simple plane of rules
like we crumpled the sheet
and that our courage, our desire,
if we'd want to,
could join anywhere.
Now we are anxiously drifting
on top of dark, stormy oceans.
We are so close to each other that
there is nothing between us.
We are sitting on a shipwreck,
on a worn-out bed
of two square meters,
I squeeze your hands, tell me,
it's not the end yet, is it?

Failure ≈ Tévedés

Like a crude god, I occasionally play with an idea,
and push the "IT WAS A FAILURE" button.
I take pleasure in seeing how cities disappear,
how streets, parks, names get deleted, how
my denial washes even the holiest gardens away.
I mock the mountains: Can you see?
How tiny mounds you all are, if I want you to be so.
I inhale the bitter vapor of my anger
and I make myself believe
that healing is a triumph.

With Wings Up ≈ Szárnyakkal fölfelé

There was a small butterfly figure on the ring,
its wings decorated by colorful gems.
Yellow curtains were rippling on the horizon,
the morning's atmosphere was festive as my
grandma came home, with my gift,
from the market of Pásztó.
The wind flew under her scarf,
just like in the following Saturday,
with the same gift-giving smile on her face
but already in the drafty mortuary
lying in her open coffin.
I've never had a ring before. It occurred to me while
playing that I should lose this miraculous object.
I longed for the pleasure,
to find it, to receive it again.
I dug a pit in the sandbox,
and I buried the ring with its wings up.
I had a hard time falling asleep,
but I got up early the next day.
I dug up the whole sandbox again and again,
and not just where I thought I hid it.
I've been looking for it for thirty-six years now
The sandbox since had overgrown with thujas.
I can't find it for over thirty-six years.
It made me anxious for thirty-six years
now I don't know who to thank
for this burden.

Appealing to Agent Scully ≈ Könyörgés Scully ügynökhöz

Agent Scully, please let me borrow your
smart eyes, your beautiful oval shaped face!
Don't let whimsical mood and sentiment
etiolate and wither the skin on my face!

Don't let me believe there's a secret life
running, an underworldly beautiful
conspiracy below the surface, give me a sign
with drawn brows: augury won't be usable!

Agent Scully, don't let it hurt me!
Let me be like you, a cool trench coat,
a headstrong mind, don't let me worry
if anyone turns into an alien in my heart.

My heart is an elderflower. If I feel
it's as a steaming plate of love,
please come and cull me, fully!

Little Zoli's Car ≈ Zolika autója

I really liked it, just like a real one.
With a little yellow shovel I dug
the tunnel of my castle in the sandbox
with great care while I was thinking
only of little Zoli's car.
Three rounds, that's what we agreed on,
up to the end of street and back.

The space in my weak and collapsible
castle widened with every grain.
He wanted to see my pussy in exchange
of the car. Pulling my panty down
to my knees, that was the deal.

The strong drink milk and matured
by victories. While I only yearned for
the toy car of little Zoli, and never endured milk.
My protein allergy's still distressing me,
just like this childhood memory.

I live in my indestructible fortress
that cannot be undermined,
and toss and turn at every dawn
before I fall back to sleep.

Either way I pedaled giving a wide berth

to the house at the street's end, the dogs
barked at me when I passed each tree three times.

I didn't know then
that for the sake of honor I shouldn't have
ever turned back to anyone.

Bellybutton Map ≈ Köldöktérkép

Look for my bellybutton toward
southwest from New York.
Then let me draw your finger to my mouth.
You can see the virgins' mountains of my heart,
only when it hurts. Where do we melt slowly
shrinking?

I've lived over here – see: afar. Are we still close?
Beyond the door, a drizzling snowfall. The white street
is still a virgin and tight. It's cold, you fool,
still I don't mind you. Let me be to you
whatever you let me be, or allow me
to figure ourselves out to you.

Shower ≈ Zuhany

Let the water run! Easy, wash your back!
Now, from shoulder to palm you're your own mother.
You don't have to become a baby though.
You could be more true, but why should you be
more of a saint? Love yourself as much
as you could hope
you still have some time to wash up
not only for yourself.
You're naked. You got neither dirt, nor perfume,
gather your strength – it's gonna be cold
so better be prepared.
Rue dims the tile and the mirror.
Pay attention to your new face, erase the old one.

In Every Rupture ≈ Minden szakadásban

Don't say I'm your mother!
The truth is getting bolder.
It squeezes. It let's go. It squeezes.
I don't sleep well.

Love will crack after it ripens.
It tastes dry, its drained
remembrance rests on the thigh.

You know the laws of my body:
Ten minutes of convulsive shaking.
Ten minutes weakness. Peace.

Silence.

Grace in every rupture.

With the Fathers ≈ Az apákkal

The problem with the fathers is
that they always betray you.
They lie that they hold you with their
hands when they teach you to walk,
that they hold the rear of the bicycle seat
and they go under the water
with you into a terrifying uncertainty,
By the time you realize they'll be at the doorpost,
or at the end of the street,
or sitting by the pool shouting go, go
and proud they taught you
how to live fucking alone

Panta Rhei ≈ Panta Rhei

1.

Panta rhei means that
everything with a name
is simply a riverbed.
In vain you nickname it.
No one ever stares at the
same feverish gaze twice

2.

Panta rhei means that
no one ever steps twice in
the same water.
The river leaving its bed
has the same inertia.

Drone Festival ≈ Drónfesztivál

In a cool mid-morning, no better fest
than the Spring fest
Family day, drone festival at the end of the village.
Small machines humming, gliding below the sky.
A speaker constantly squawking into the mic:
"Crop circles are made by helicopters heads down!"
Huge line in front of the fighter simulator
three minutes for an inverted life,
for innocent maneuvers,
for a harmless fall.
A guy's pushing raffle tickets.
I shake him off with a lie.

Out of thin air a group of white storks
returning home flew right into
the smell of meat stew whipped up to the sky.
With motionless wings
they disappear to the left on
the horizon with majestic weariness.

Resurrection ≈ Feltámadás

The Mediterranean villa is located
on the corner of Libatop Street.
Sloped roof, whitewashed pseudo-stone walls,
marble tile driveway. Up in the terrace, the glass door
is staring at the sea. End of March,
the palm trees have been
shoved into the sun. They graze in deep mortars
in the light. The only thing that's missing
is the sea to lie about.
The arable land with the electric
poles is now the infinite.
This Spring breeze belongs to the daily resurrection.
The mixed-breed dog of the temporary neighbor
sips from muddy puddles and
with a muzzy, translucent
face, reminiscent of you,
it urinates a golden yellow arch
on the fence's ornaments.

The Time of My Life ≈ The Time of My Life

Rideau Lakes, Ontario, Canada.
Maple forests, leaf litter squeaking
from zealous worms
Again in the land of wailing loons.
As far as the eye can see: lakes.
Tiny Islands.
Forests on the land, forests,
as if they grew out of the water.
Osprey nests on the bent branches of pine trees.
Deer in the clearings.
Inverse squirrels among the boughs
(black body, red tail).
Rat snakes at the bottom of the grass
and frogs of all kinds.
Millipedes on the muddy dirt road.
A large, red headed woodpecker resembling a ghost
rustles among the trees,
drumming, pecking.

Over here, everything is as if it's the first
sunny Sunday afternoon
after the flood.

At nights, the loons are wailing on the lake
over a sunken world.
Their wailings are deceiving,
not at all mourning lamenting.
It's mating season, they're lovers.
"I'm having the time of my life, the time of my life"

That's what they scream into the dark night.
There isn't any change at the research station,
Cobwebs on the doors, smell of
mold and cold in the house.
It's as if nothing had happened in a year.
The days turn to other days unnoticed.
The weather is idyllic.
The food at the canteen is tolerable,
I chit-chat with others
after eating. Then I walk down to the harbor
and catch some fish
or amble over to the marsh
to check out the beaver dam.

On occasion I visit Chaffey's Lock.
It's a local attraction, a sluice.
The little bridge is rolled up twice a day,
to allow boats to pass between
the two lakes with different names.

There is a level difference between the two lakes,
the ships are first diverted into a channel.
There the sluice is locked behind them and
slowly opening the other one at the end of the channel
to allow water to flow in or out until
it's is enough and
the water level reaches the level of the other lake
and the ships can swim smoothly over.
If I'm utterly bored of ourselves
I drive to the closest library,
or store in Elgin, to a tiny,
charmingly insignificant village,
to get this and that,

a mushroom field guide,
movies,
milk,
crackers,
cocoa.

I like driving over here,
the nearest destination is twenty minutes
via lavish landscapes.
I turn the CD player on while driving
Kispál and the Borz is in for two months already.
That's what I listen to,
the same CD since April.
Drumming on the wheel,
singing loudly like teenager.
When the "Jutka swam across the river" tune comes
I pump up the volume and cry.
I have no one here
I have no one here
I have no one here like the way
you are not here for me.

I cry until it ends.
I either get full or
get emptied out.
Then, life can go on.

Pupil ≈ Tanítvány

I took him to a nearby cliff.
The old sea lies deep below.
Other times I stand there all alone.

I thoroughly explained everything
about the momentum and
the push off,
how to listen in the fall
in the hissing silence between the two worlds.

how to retain himself,
his breath, that is he, life,
and to pay close attention to what
the soul is holding on to
when diving under the water,

that his old world will close and turn
dark above him
his heartbeat drums on his eardrum
until he falls asleep in the infinite,

those few moments before breaking the surface
for air because the desire has gone
from the lungs, the will to live,
are the most important.
Those few seconds in the chill of death.

I thoroughly explained that to him,
like a mother, and older sister

I inculcated in him: jump, never fall,
only if there is no other way but forward

alright then, now, he replied
I thought it over, considered it
as he stood at the edge of the cliff
he immediately began to unbutton his shirt

are you crazy? I screamed at him,
you cannot be, cannot be ready yet,
I feared for him, as a child, a brother,
but I was rather afraid he would
reveal his naked soul before me
then what will I hold on to suddenly.

Nostalgia ≈ Nosztalgia

𝄢

The airplane turns into position, the pilot
is ready to take off. The engines begin to roar,
the asphalt starts to run and with a sudden jerk
the way the band-aid or wax strips from a woman's leg
your country peels away from you.

𝄢

You fall asleep above the mirror of the ocean.
Were you wake up, the new world,
was built with familiar symbols.
You can easily orient yourself to roads, lights and
faces.
You don't understand the mountains, afraid of rivers
still occasionally you find refuge in them
looking for familiar thighs and swirls.

𝄢

Counterparts keep you alive.
In a certain section the New River below Radford
is just like the Danube by Budakalász.
The elderly woman next door has
bone cancer, left Hungary in '56,
reminds you of your mother.

𝄢

You know, over here, the pain
immediately hits the bone.
The water at home, would heal me, I believe,
The air at home, my room I've left not saying
goodbye, my mother's never seen funeral.
Talked about the real summers at Lake Balaton,
the streets of Budapest.
nurses rustling, changing the sheets,
until we run out of the slowly falling days.

𝄢

You'll get home in years. When your plane lands
it's welcomed with champagne and jets of water.
Yours was the 100th anniversary flight.
My little country - you mutter to yourself -
My little country, as it's been written, you see ?
your son is coming home!

You smile when you clearly read fucking asshole
from the mouth of the honking driver next to you.
Later you'll become careful.

𝄢

You're embracing each Hungarian word for weeks.
You build a house in a street
which has neither name nor pavement.

𝄢

Again a few years slip by.
Unsustainable road conditions.
You walk home by detour.
Your mother gets ill.

𝄢

One morning you wake up to see your face
as a dried-up sea of mud.
You'd talk to someone, in Hungarian,
but you're not in the mood.
After unfolded days you bury your head in the pillow
and realize how staggeringly you crave
that distant country you left
behind next to a deathbed.
Patting your pillow at length as
if you were building a nest
to the irrevocable rooflessness
circling above your head.

Endre Ady, Föl földobott kő, poem

35

Life is Pink ≈ Az élet rózsaszín

Life, well, is bold.
See? Like the mold
behind the bed on the wall:
sin, and woe is always recurring.

Life, well, is bitter,
the heart does hammer, flutter,
in our closed vessels
time is ever running addled.

Sometime, life is familiar,
like a song
that began with a cue
and is heard ever strong.
(what short of music is this?)

Life is pale
—you might even think—
those who saw a dead body
say it's pink.

I'm Not a Poet ≈ Nem vagyok költő

I'm not a poet, I simply like going to cafes.
Enjoy a few lonely minutes,
sitting and watching what hangs out
from the world while it puts on airs.

My husband thinks I have a lover.
The neighbor thinks I keep money in
a secret Swiss account or another.
Instead, I pack in and out of an
empty closet every morning,
cook, wash and yell at the kids
like my mother did.

An overloaded van spilled corn
in front of me this morning.
(I was simply going shopping.)
The gold poured out.
I passed him in the roundabout.
I had to cry and I got lost in the parking lot.

Amphibian ≈ Kétéltű

What is this creature? Never see it at day light.
Hiding as leaf, stone, tree branch.
Don't know where it lives, don't know how it lives.
but I know it singled me out once.

It visits me at night, wakes me up:
Man builds the church to he wrong spot!
Then it drags me to the lake by the church.

Lies down on the bottom of the lake. Hugs me.
Its chest is soft mud, its desire seaweed.
The stirred up time slowly subsides around us.
the minutes feather down in the dunes.
What's waiting for me is another world,
I forget to spring into existence

To a Mole ≈ Egy vakondhoz

I'm having a seemingly fruitless
dialogue with a mole for days.
What it carries to the world,
the dark, loose heap of earth,
the dirt of its scary dreams,
I harrow during the day.
I don't ask what sorrow
constantly chasing it to wander
down in the underworld.
It doesn't ask what hope
gives life to my garden.
This is how we tease each other
day and night,
night and day,
as if the evergreen, dark
deep hearth of my yard
would never go to waste.

Long Winter ≈ Hosszú tél

It's quiet and white again.
You're long gone, prints of cat feet remain.
It's melting. The sidewalk sparkles behind you.
I read your footprints, mud lies under the snow.

I watch the sky, what shall it bring today,
while I put on the already cold coffee.
I warm myself: should I find you in the coffee ground?
what would I learn in your yesterday?

I know well, there is no lie between us.
Only icicles, your silence between two drops.
humiliate me boldly: hush – see I'm silent.
By tomorrow you will be forgotten once more.

By a Hair's Breadth ≈ Hajszálnyira

I've learned to accept your affairs and your body.
Whoever you love is like your arms or legs to you.
Sitting in your car I see myself
as a hungry mouth that wants to
kiss your neck, ears, yet all my yearning left to itself.
You turned the heat up beforehand
so I wouldn't catch a cold
when you stop somewhere.
I'm thinking of pieces of hair, blond,
brown that you couldn't get rid of
from the back seat despite your
striving when for a few minutes
I became irrevocably yours.

Junk Watches ≈ Bóvli órák

It seems to me that at the corner canteen
the menu is always the same since the beginning.
You sit across from me, I sit across from you,
and the whole thing reminds of an old stanza.

No wonder the Gods got bored of this world.
Show me an acceptable tragedy!
To me, who was left on the roadside alive,
a worthwhile love affair, cry insanity—

oh, whatever you saw on Monday I saw Friday,
so stop talking when the curtain call is the same!

But I saw you, you were there when
the curtain was torn in two.
So you can trust me and I know I can trust you
since we are sitting in the canteen from the beginning
during this anno domini hungry and thirsty hour
not knowing what our roles might be
with these junk watches on our wrists. . . . Listen.
Ticking: we two   we two   we two.

At Least ≈ Legalább

Here I lie in shame
nothing covers me
before you dissect me
corpse scalpel am I
to you until death
at least admit that
stubborn heart,
my bloodstream's
most beautiful

in vain I tried to
puke out your absence
my coiling bowels relish
the poison of your flavor
at least let me cool off
on the edges of your mouth
sing me away slowly
cut me up or write me newly

To my Mirror ≈ Tükrömhöz

I don't care about the tantrum of the body.
What they tell me face to face,
that it's over, it doesn't exist, I want to
know where the words are falling!

Sentiment is a gaudy woven, delicate web,
my mind is the sticky wall of my blood vessel.
Can they fall over a wound? That's beyond me.
If I step aside not to be an obstacle?

The soul might be a cave. A vault,
it shapes distorted statues—the word is alluvium.
They dribble aimlessly.
It's over. There is nothing. Nothing.
When they fall they strike a cold, silent lake.

By Morning ≈ Mire reggel

While the day lasts
it sits on the ledge.
I fall asleep, unfold
and darken inside.

It's not waiting, isn't scared,
it only flies.
Inside it breaks, crushes
its blood isn't tamed.

The morning is a dead bird.

Basement Window ≈ Pinceablak

Our family's past in ankle height –
a basement window, though without glass
it's rather a hole – wide space above –
paved streets and summer.
Sometimes the ice cream cart rings this way.

Eight people hunkering down, I feel the shivering
of my great-uncles my sister and little daddy
by my ankle. Bombs are dropped. Cold air escapes.
Broken shadow of man trembles on the wall.
My brother, you're alive? They embrace,
cry, laughter then silence follows.

Can you hear the stretching of the spiderless webs?
Can you see how deep is the cavity behind them?
by god, my son, don't get to close to that!
What guards and what awaits is equally motionless.

46

Capturing Prisoners ≈ Foglyul ejteni

I like to walk where the trees, the stones
and the dense vegetation entwine high noon,
which would simply run away, but gets stuck,
falls in a trap. As a scented shadow, time
oozes inside the erratic cracks of the stones.
Smell of good wine and must: the secret of
existence guarded by fruit flies is settling.

I'm a small child, I'm standing by
the quarry stone wall of our old house
and staring at my palm,
trying to smell the depth of
the unfamiliar lines.
Then I began to see how the afternoon
fades and darkens away, evaporates
from the bed of my destiny to the
odorless, tasteless eternity
that's reminiscent of nothing.

Should ≈ Kellene

You should be standing on top of the planet,
see it for a long time where the sky is,
earth, the boundaries,
reread every book letter by letter,
you should know all those who're dying
and all the newborns by name.

you should squat on the deepest bottom of the sea,
decipher from the reverse what fate is, your desire,
should explain to a child, where God lives,
and where the animals.

Figure out how much you worth,
but don't get discouraged,
let a sigh change body, sing, dance,
but watch for the rhythm, were the line ends,
oh, you poor, you fool twenty first century!

Be Careful with Imagination! ≈ **Óvatosan a képzelgéssel!**

Be careful with imagination!
If you're anxious in your desire,
never again expect the one,
who secretly awaits with budding surprise,
if you prise open her thighs,
if you screw her, the angel to death!

Be careful with imagination! Never think of evil.
You ain't strong. If you summon him, the Satan,
the evil dog will break loose. Conjure him only
when you're sure you've got balls,
to bite him up with tooth and nail, to eat his heart out!

ZITA IZSÓ

ARRIVAL

A Long-Time-No-See Relative ≈ Rég nem látott rokon

He's sitting at the groaning board,
their only child on his lap.
Now he's squatting on the street and,
like a folding chair,
he's leaning against a wall.
I let him stay with me a while,
then he moved into one of my T-shirts.
In the store I last saw him.
the security guard asked him to open his bag,
to show that it was empty.

Then he laughed, as if to show
that there were no words in his mouth.

As the Offspring of the Cichlids
≈ Ivadékaikat a bölcsőszájú halak

I mostly remember the snow.
We elbowed on the windowsill,
staring at the infinite whiteness
when the soldiers broke the door in.
I had just enough time
to drag my little sister to the pantry.
While we were hiding
each breath hurt as if a
bayonet was stabbing me.
I worried that it could pierce
between my ribs.
Then it was over.
They'll find us, my little sister screamed.
I squeezed my eyes shut so as
not to see what they would do to her.
It's said that in the greatest need
one can hear God's voice.
Perhaps you don't speak, my Lord,
because you don't carry us
in the palm of your hand, but in your mouth,
the way-cichlids carry their offspring.
The soldiers dragged me out to the garden,
spread my legs.
stuffed snow in my mouth to stifle my weird,
prolonged scream. At first I didn't
know it came from me. I thought
a rat got stuck between
the insulation and the roof, squealing,
struck its head until it was bloody and stuck.

54

But when the soldiers stuffed my mouth with snow
I realized the sound came from me.
The snow melted,
the slush dripping down my throat.
It tasted like the falling snow
my little sister and
I caught on our tongues.
Since the war began
nothing tastes the same,
not my mother's soup,
not my granny's sponge cake.
But the taste of snow didn't change at all.
My mother said God carries us
in the palm of His hand,
not in His mouth.
Lying on the cold ground,
I am thinking of the warmth of your palm, my Lord.
When the soldiers finished, they stood up,
said nothing, remained silent.
The mountains drill the sky
the way teeth bite the lips
of a man suppressing a cry.

Fish from the family Cichlidae.

Arrival ≈ Érkezés

Those who saw her father's face knew
that the real home   wouldn't be familiar.
You wouldn't find the toy you lost
in the field when you were seven.
Your far-away pets wouldn't be there either,
nor the drawing you accidentally tore,
after which you cried for a long time.

Still, you will not miss anything.
Besides, nothing will be in vain.
Time won't pass unnoticed anymore,
like flour spilled from
a torn bag.

Your mother will be there and sit you on her knee,
and, as if you fell asleep watching a movie,
she tells you
how your life would have gone on
if you hadn't died.

What's going to be weird is
that you'll find it hard to recall
how your features used to look.
You're afraid you'll forget your face
the way you forget
a relative you haven't seen
for a long time.
Then you look around,
recognize yourself in the things around you,
recognize your back's curve

in the tree that leans over the river,
the color of your hair in
the bark peeled-from its trunk,
by then because you'll be in everything.

And fear will never find its way into you again.

Fish Soup ≈ Halleves

When he came towards me I knew
what it meant.
I wanted to cook fish soup,
but quickly turned off the gas
so as not to burn myself
if I fell.
He was shouting,
saying I've talked to everyone again.
My smile is indecent,
like a fly left open,
and in vain he's shaking a rattle.
He can't keep the angels away from the fruit.
I'm too good for everyone,
so nothing remains for him.

Our kitchen was small
like a too-early confession.
The two of us could barely move around in it.
He was coming toward me. I picked up a knife.

I had to chop the vegetables into tiny pieces
so they would cook thoroughly,
because his teeth were bad,
could have broken into harsh words
he would throw at me
if he didn't like the meal.

Then he ran into to it.
The doctor said I stabbed him,
but I don't remember.

I was standing with
the knife in my hand.
When I bought it
the salesman said it would not cut
root vegetables well
if the blade's edge became dull.

I didn't have money to buy a new one
and I don't have a good knife to cut
with and I must swallow everything
because of the children.
Because he staggered
I called an ambulance

His eyes widened
as if he began to see
the people around him
for the first time,
as if the outside world began to fill him
like water seeping into a sinking ship.

Meanwhile the children
rushed in from the garden
saying my shouting scared them
because they thought I had been killed.

Now I can't speak,
as if my mouth was stuffed
with raw vegetables
that I can't chew
because they are

coarsely chopped

and not thoroughly cooked.

Many sympathize with me,
but I'm afraid of being acquitted
because it will be said that, behold, freedom.
You can go now.
But then I will have to learn to walk again.
In vain I cling to the chair.
It will tilt in our home
and the cane will break,
the floor disintegrates under my feet.
Everything proves to be soft and weak.
Since he is not here now
the world became flexible.

I don't know where the walls are.
I feel like a living fish
carried in a plastic bag.
I can't talk about these
matters with anyone.
I blame myself only,
and I dream about him,

dreams that never came true.
For instance, while stroking my arms he says
he had never eaten such delicious soup—
all the flavors of the world—
an entire Atlantis of flavors swam in my fish soup.

He keeps spooning the submerged civilization,
a garden bordered by a hedge,
a whitewashed house,
and our life, which started so happy.

Silk ≈ Selyem

I might have truly wanted it,
or at least it was my fault,
since my mother said
that a woman should dress properly.
During recess
I was cold in the school yard
so I asked if I could go inside.
He said
make yourself useful,
go with him to the supply closet,
help pack things away.
Then he asked me
to roll up the map
and don't think about the world
which would condemn us.

As he stepped closer
I was watching the window.
I saw
a tree branch hitting the glass
in the strong wind
and I waited to see
which thrust
would finally break it.

We've rarely met outside of school.
We only got together on the beach sometimes.
I knew when I was inside
he wouldn't dare go to the water

and I could leave him for good.
If I swam across the world,
surely I'd find some clothes someone left
on the other side.
I'd put them on
and I wouldn't have to feel
naked all the time.

One day my mother told me
that she thinks boys don't look at me
because I don't wax my legs,
but she'll do it for me.
I shouldn't worry, it'll hurt a bit.
It's not simply thing
to be a woman.
As she stripped the wax sheets from my legs
I felt she was pulling off my skin
and with it his touches.
From then on
I felt much cleaner
when something hurt.

My mother was so happy
she gave me her silk stockings,
put them on.
She leaned back with great satisfaction
as if she had eaten all the chocolate,
pastries, and candies
which she didn't buy
so she could fit in those stockings.
She was so happy,
she dabbed
her perfume on my hair.

Its scent was still on me
and when I met him.
I felt as if my mother
stood behind me;
That made me freeze.

He shouted at me,
what do you think,
think yourself pretty,
and why do I wear such things?
So he tore the stockings off.
I knew my mother would blame me
for not taking care of them.

She'll tell me
she shouldn't have bought
me such beautiful dresses.
She'd better
use my clothes for dusting.
She should wash the
windows with my blouse,
blow her nose in my skirt.

I imagined
her doing that and
all became ligher.

Since then, it doesn't hurt when he lies on me,
his chest not pressing my bones
as if I didn't have a body,
all of me light and soft,
mere velvet, cotton, damask, and silk.

The Last Request ≈ **Az utolsó kérés**

Darkness and light will once again mingle
like the colors of my mother's hair dyes.
Giant water creatures
swim within the skulls of those who are dying
to bring relief with the cool strokes of their fins.
Birds fly back to hatch
their eggs they laid on other planets.
For the last time plants overgrow everything
that we could never forget.

Then everything we love will be gone.
We'll be like
empty terrariums with the light left on,
fibers of desire
still illuminated.

We, who despite the warnings,
trying to survive,
watch a nature film
of species long extinct
and when we see the last common crane
we cry as if it were our child
who we are too old to raise.

Later, almost every evening
the building super knocks on the door
and asks if we have enough to eat.
Our night will be calm
and uneventful,

like the life of a distant relative
who wouldn't move anywhere.
If we reason with her to get up
she only repeats
that it's not necessary to cook for one person.
No one will be afraid.
No one will huddle
or hold another's hand.
That distant relative will be there.
Still she wouldn't move a bit.
She'll only uses the words she speaks for cooking—
pour it in the pot,
add some of this and
a pinch of that,
mix it,
thicken it,
stir it.
All the while we keep our
hands behind our backs.
Everything we have.
All of our own lives.

Inner Solar System ≈ Belső naprendszer

While you go from hospital to hospital
and cry when you see a newborn,

The hospital staff tells you to
listen to everyone.
Let their words, like little eggs, nest
in the fissures of your heart.

Hatching as larvae, they will buzz around you
like the dust particles that make up Saturn's ring.

Then you'll believe
that you too are a planet
having all the conditions for life.
And one day the doctors will make
you habitable as well.

Silence ≈ Némaság

For an instant after waking
you don't recall what gravitation is.

But soon enough you recognize
the worn furniture
in the dim light,

and then remember
that Julius Caesar's soldiers
burned the Great Library of Alexandria,
and man in the rock-cut tomb had been dead
for three days already.

You are as lonely
as if you were alone in the Garden of Eden.
In vain you've improved much.
In vain you have developed good qualities,
but if no one is there to acknowledge them,

you feel like
a plant
which became extinct
before it was discovered.

It would feel good if someone would be happy for you.
You imagine an alien whose face lies like a politcian's
when he smiles at the year's first newborns.

When you get up,
you won't be waiting for His Creation any longer.

You recreate yourself each morning
using whatever substance is handy,
though you haven't looked in the mirror for weeks
so you don't know how you look.

You sit up.
It sounds as if someone is
crying behind the walls,
but it's only in your head.
It's hard to accept
that everything that exists is
with you in this room.

Ice ≈ Jég

When he hit me, my mother
locked herself in the bathroom
and turned on the water.
It ran for so long
that I saw the whole river Danube
flowing through the tap
like apologetic sentences in his ears.

Why he hit me, I had to figure out.
If I couldn't, he hit me harder.
He crushed burning cigarettes on my skin,
threw empty soda cans at me then
crushed them on the floor
my relatives, friends, coaches,
who would help me.

His liked to say,
"you're a dike, a rug muncher."
He squeezed my hand with the strength of
a dead animal's locked jaws.
Sometimes he woke me in the middle of the night
and beat me locked me out of the house,
me wearing only pajamas.
He said, "You have to be tough."
I got used to pain.
My wounds multiplied like tooth marks
on bones thrown to stray dogs.
I was free only when I skated on ice.
He couldn't touch me.

The Direction of Current ≈ A sodrás iránya

"Did you know that this is a river, too?"
you asked, and I didn't answer,
but felt as it went through me,
like objects that can be easily moved,
uncertain decisions,
temporary sensations.

The point where we touched
before your illness
found the deepest basin,
and—according to my notions—
where we were joined together as
twins before we were born.

A mother with a river flowing inside hears a burbling
the doctors say happens from high blood pressure.

But that's
what children hear as talk
in their mother's belly

They say I'm more restrained nowadays.

We who carry a river inside
move carefully
to prevent the waves from splashing,
avoid sudden moves to keep
anything slipping from our mouths

that others don't expect,

like what the doctor said
about your condition.

We prefer to stay unnoticed,
since we grew up with this river inside our bodies
and we grow cold quickly
the way statues might
when they realize their own nakedness.

The truth is I don't dare to look deep inside.

I'm not worried about the river, but its current.
I'm trying to deny its course,
I tell myself you won't die.
Every illness can be cured
and we'll always be happy.

I'm trying to believe this.
I say completely different things in my dreams like,
"you don't have to fight for
me if you don't want to""
and trust yourself to the current."

But these are truly not my words.
I can't hold them back for
when I sleep the river flows
to the pillow from my mouth.

The News ≈ A hír

I was in the pastry shop
when my phone rang.
I picked it up on only the second ring
because I still had to pay at the counter
so I could bring you your favorite pastry.
After I heard the news
all I could think was that the pastry
will be edible for three days.
These three days are my only chance.
In three days the news may turn out to be false.
It wasn't you, and there was no death,
and those who we covered with earth
will shake their bodies, dust off their clothes,
sit at the table and say
that it's lucky they got home before the storm,
because they didn't have their coats with them,
though this won't explain their long absence.

Fakir ≈ Fakír

𝄢

Her last memory from Aleppo was the fakir.
He knelt on a blanket and was eating broken glass.
Nothing happened to him, though the shards hurt his
throat.
For a few weeks after the stunt he didn't speak.

𝄢

Soon after, the siege began.
The women and children could do nothing
so they rearranged the apartment every two days.
The men stumbled into the displaced furniture
every night when they came home.
The parents bickered more and more.
Slowly, they devoured each other,
a species of fish in an aquarium
who have been without food too long.

The siege lasted a month,
the family living behind drawn curtains.
Three days and three hundred nights went by
When, in spite of her mother's warning, she went out.
Her parents, brothers, and sisters were sleeping.
She saw an enormous light.
A blast threw her several meters.
When she saw the destroyed house
she remembered being frightened

when she was separated from
her parents in a museum.
She cried for hours then,
but now didn't feel anything.
She stared at the ruins and the broken window glass
and thought if she cut herself now it wouldn't hurt.
She had to be dragged from there.
When later people asked her what had happened
she didn't answer for a long time,
as if she had eaten broken glass.

With Your Back to the Sea ≈ A tengernek háttal

Your companions drowned.

After seven days you wake,
hearing their cries.
Your dreams are like the sea.
Your friends' mismatched shoes
drift inside you,
like debris in a sunken ship.
Sleeping, you see
hands growing out of water,
moving like tree branches in the wind
Light blinds everything
and you want to run into the water
to save your friends,
but it strikes you that you're a coward.
This is when you usually wake up.
You search for someone to talk to,
carefully though, so what you say
won't seem apologetic.
You hope that the outpouring of words
will tear down your sense of reality,
the way waves wash away
futile and inaccessible shores.

Awakening ≈ Ébredés

It's still dark.
The first sunrise after creation
could be like the museum galleries
attendants walk through—
the corridors empty before opening—
and turn on the lights.

I open my eyes.
You are the first person
I see.
I wonder
how long it will take
me to tell you apart from other creatures,
realizing you didn't grow out of the moss
you are standing on.
You are not fallen fruit.

To distinguish you from other creatures
I need to watch.
Yet, what now I see in the sky
is not the sun,
but a planet
that lights things
we cannot believe exist.

Sleeping Exercises ≈ Alvásgyakorlatok

I'm tired.
I want to sleep, but I'm
like a sinking cargo vessel.
There is time to leave the deck
and everything that steered me
until now.
I run out of thoughts.
I turn the TV on and
wars break out.
Someone pours garbage into a creek in the woods.
Elsewhere a newborn puppy is set on fire.
and as tree crowns catch plastic bags
thoughts others want to forget
get caught in my mind.

Then I think about you—
that I'm still awake, while
you are surely sleeping
behind thick curtains.
Dreaming about me.
I don't want to be anything else
in these few hours
but myself.
Before I was afraid of living,
but now I close my eyes.
When as children out of curiosity
we stuffed dry plaster in our mouths,
chewed cardboard,
I sensed I was alive.

My limbs feel heavy.
I sleep. In my dream I am a fox
caged in a zoo,
happy imagining
itself the first fox
the kid who is watching has ever seen.

Sinking ≈ Merülés

You talk about friends,
your words like carnivorous beetles
the London Museum staff
cleans animal bones with.
You would rather wash
your friends' bones with water.
But it was them
who whispered poisoned rivers
into your ears.

As you grew older, your friends
ordered you out of love the way
adults ordered you out from
of the quickly cooling water
of Lake Balaton
when you were a child.

After you talk about this.
you dream that you go to the beach.
People stuffed you with candies
and you put sand in your mouth
to keep from vomiting.
It will take years
for you to throw up all the shit
you were stuffed with
the way the sea does,
the way a sunken ship
disgorges its cargo.

Dividing ≈ Osztódás

Changing currents dragged a fish to shore.
A house you imagined
when you were a child
would fit in its stomach.
You stood beside the fish and cried,
because you had no children
to help push it back into the sea.

They say you must carry on regardless.
That's how it is.
Think about your parents,
grandparents. They live inside you,
but you think of the giant grebe
which became extinct the year
you were born.

You say
you'll keep a room inside yourself.
If you succeed in growing
the tree in your front yard
and its roots reach the depth
where the dead are buried,
you will talk about ancestors
who needed as much air as the tree produces
each year to live.

At the end
you'll see two fish before you.
Swimming inside you,
they will compete.

You promised
you would not name them
even after they are born
because they would realize
that they were separated
and would never forgive you for that.

The Final Judgment ≈ Utolsó ítélet

I didn't see you lose consciousness,
but imagined
your outstretched hand fell beside your body,
like a bird hitting a window it didn't see.
Even if you can't see us, you-feel our presence.
Our images appear before you,
the way shadows of swimmers flicker
on the sea floor.
On the midday news I heard that
a district nearby was evacuated
while a bomb from an old war
which had not exploded,
was disarmed.
The camera showed the vacated apartments
and stores where in vain we searched for your body.

The landscape might be like this at the end of the
world.
I worried
that soon the One with the Power will arrive,
and the dead will rise.
But you, you sleep away.

Quarantine ≈ Karantén

You hoped
that when the pandemic is over
the world would be cleaner,
as if the streets were freshly mopped floors.
Before, you didn't dare go out for weeks.
Well surely, we'll forget this time,
like we've forgotten the days in Paradise
or our first three years of life.

Then you think of beginning again,
the way kids excitedly
tell each other how they
spent their summer vacations.
 Instead -you lie about
what you dreamt last night.

By the time you go out you'll be like a god
who has to be recreated
based on the leftover statues
after the end of the world.

You don't have to wait
until all your cells are replaced.
After all, you'll be resurrected
and can be yourself easily,
since no one remembers
that you had ever lived.

Melting ≈ Olvadás

Because of climate change
bears wake up prematurely from their winter sleep.
Our dead wake up before their time, too,
because we can't make peace with them at the right
time.
In vain they try, but they can't go back to sleep.
They don't feel anything anymore,
but when they were hungry
they knock over the garbage cans
and scatter the garbage we accumulated
over the decades
We won't turn on the lights
so they won't see us.
We watch them from behind
the misted window glass,
knowing this is our last chance
to talk to them.
Still, we don't dare to go out
worrying that
we won't be able to tame them anymore.

Aftershock ≈ Utórengés

Birds wait on the shore.
A fish swam close to the surface—
which made me wonder,
does my face show that I'm thinking of you?
I'm thinking that it didn't really end at the end,
but when I waited for you for hours in vain,
to keep myself busy
I watched the news on a muted TV
in an appliance store window.
I saw the faces of earthquake survivors
and from then on I knew
I'd never be able to talk about you.
I stood there before the smeared glass,
munching on sugar-candied peanuts
I brought for you
while they broadcast pictures of
the churches of the oldest gods fall.
It wasn't hard to imagine
how I will forget you.
Since then, sometimes you march across my face
like the news ticker scrolls
at the bottom of the TV screen,
or vibrating neon signs
above the entrance of closed stores.
Men tell me I talk in my sleep.
That's when you surface in me,
like air bubbles from a sinking ship.
When I awake I can't remember anything,
yet live in the time zone of our common life.
When my phone rings I always hope it's

you who is calling.
When someone knocks, I hope you're
standing at the door,
like an animal after an earthquake who
listens to every human word
as if they were its name.

Expulsion ≈ Kiűzetés

We are walking in silence,
you behind me,
not talking about yourself.
Across the street a little child starts singing.
I feel in her voice that she doesn't
know the song's end.

I'm not asking,
rather wondering
if your secrets are in my possession already,
like last year's chestnuts in my pocket.
I had no idea what to do with them then and still don't.

Then we sat facing each other
as if to prove that we are not afraid of things
like spikes on a fence that
would pierce us
if we let them
into our imaginations.
We haven't said a word since we got on our way.
We used to think it didn't matter whether

we kept silent
or talked.

But an unfamiliar bird
settled in a tree
and we knew
its name will be
the first word we will utter.

Degrees of Faith   ≈   A hit fokozatai

I can't talk about the arrival.
Imagine your stretch of coast,
a glass upside down, and a window view of the sea.
Every day, someone comes out of the water who was
dying in another part of the world.
Over here he stands on one leg, tilts his head, hops,
lets the water run from his ears.
Yet eye movement, renal contraction, the onset
of circulation are not considered resurrection.

Who knows in what part of the world I shall find you?
Will I be there when you walk out of the water?
Will you be angry with me for not calling your name,
for letting you walk around, sit, tired, hungry.
You'll get accustomed to the body's desires,
to living again.
Then I'll stand before you and offer what I brought
you, its weight straining my arms.

I haven't left here for days.
I watch the harbor. The ships rock like
the pendant I gave you—a gift—
on your falling and rising chest.
At first the coastal people looked at me with interest.
Now they stare
not knowing why the legends
of the sea people don't delight me—
as if I keep an animal as a pet
which others raise for meat.

Absolution ≈ Eloldozás

We lie face-down in the sand,
hardly believing we've reached the shore,
don't know how many are safe,
how many dead.
Our features hold some terrible fear
coming from an inhuman force,
the way fresh asphalt
preserves the tracks of fleeing animals.
Then we saw the sky.
The clouds looked like
crumbs of hand-torn bread.
The rocks shine,
and the teeth glisten from saliva.
Birds try to hatch rocks.
All want to live,
yet, we'll no longer mourn those
who threw their watches into the sea
after reaching a rocky shore,
because we've learned about that short-lived,
peaceful perplexity
which any might feel when reaching the light—
like people who, coming out of the water,
can't find their clothes on the shore.
First they look for their own bodies,
then run to what they think is home,
not caring about their nakedness.

Identity ≈ Azonosság

Arriving from different countries, people tried
to comfort each other at the reception station.

They realized
they didn't have to love each other.
It would be enough to pick up two stones
of the same size.
When they are apart from each other
they wouldn't have to remember the other's name.
They will know that somewhere
someone has a similar stone,
no matter how much it hurts.

They didn't smash a window with it,
didn't talk to it, didn't wrap it up,
didn't break any heads with it.
They carry it with them just the way the others do
and feel it's weight less and less as time goes by.

KRISZTINA RITA MOLNÁR

REPORT

Hesitant Classified ≈ Tétova apró

I have never tried this strategy.
I'm not about it.
Precisely so. Just the point.
I've never searched for a man before.
He would be in his fifties.
It doesn't matter if he's widowed or divorced,
but he must have fathered a child.
Thus, he is a father who had a home once,
made a nest. (I wouldn't mind if he planted
a tree and wrote a book. According to the Chinese
those are a man's four most important things to do).
So, child, book, tree, and nest.
I wouldn't want anything else.
But please, don't send me picture
with either a pike or a jeep,
nor the wild waters he sails every
summer on his ship.
I'm looking for one who likes gardening,
who endures silence and sometimes noise.
I'm looking for someone who tells the truth
and covers me gently with a patchwork quilt
in the evenings.
But no.
I'm not looking at all.
If he wants me, find me after all.
Something about me? No. I won't say a bit.
If he'll find me, recognize me,
then get to know me.

Solution ≈ Oldás

Where I live
the crows aren't coming in the morning.
But sometime in late afternoon when time
cease to exist the way it usually does,
a flock of augurs shoots down
in black dresses
to steal timelessness.
Scaring the Angel of Evanescence,
invented by a monk,
with scabrous predictions,
Yet, the angel doesn't mind
dissolving in my tea
in the glare of winter's end.

Perhaps it's the absence
of nuts that brings
a flock of crows together.
Walnut trees aren't planted in
the gardens nowadays because
according to old beliefs
their leaves are poisonous.
There are no parks over here either.

It'll be different in February.
Spotted-breasted fieldfares are coming
to gormandize the frostbitten rowanberry.

Pigeon ≈ Galamb

Yesterday a pigeon flew above me.
There's nothing interesting in that,
but it cawed.
Was its voice false or its image?
Why is a crow covered with
pigeon's feathers?
Why didn't it coo properly,
monotonically, evenly,
as expected of a good pigeon?
What was it afraid of?
What did it warn me about?
Enough, enough.
Don't send me more warning signs.

After, Before ≈ Után, előtt

This is the time
after wars and before wars.
We're drinking tea at dusk.

𝄢

It will happen when
my doctor will shout at me, smiling,
Courage!—
though we both
are tied to a pole

waiting for the slow death by fire.
He won't know that I pray for him also,
hoping that God, to whom I'm talking,
won't be shocked
that I've asked a Buddhist monk
to heal my wounds.

𝄢

First the common poppy days,
then stars are scattered
in a poppy-seed colored night.

As in Other Times ≈ Ahogyan más időkben

As in a storm on board a ship,
the boiler rumbles and roars.
Yet there is no storm.
The fog falls all evening
as in better times
blessing falls on everything.
Yet there isn't any blessing.
Everything had frozen by morning.
Only sleet was falling,
covering us all with armor
as in hard times,
as if it were war.

Yet there is no war,
for the dead streets are sparkling,
as if in a Danish tale,
the way a spark glitters.
As it shines and glitters wickedly,
it's that kind of Danish story.
The spark penetrates your heart,
but who knows where will it go?

And will cover everything with ice,
and that nice tulip tree
I see the tree from the window,
as it bravely stands it all.

A few leaves hang proudly on its branches
for what it received

like mothers holding every
saved infant in their arms.
Yet there aren't any mothers,
nor women, nor frozen wood.
But God save them from
the tin-gray sieve of fog.

My thoughts won't let me sleep.
The boiler screams with the cold
as in other times the angel
fights wielding a flaming sword.

Batten ≈ Keresztléc

It will be done.
Right there on the window,
emptiness cut in to pieces.
What am I?
It doesn't matter.
Or not much.

Letter from the Shore of a Fjord
≈ Levél egy fjord partjáról

You know, I would rather like to burn it.
No, not out of anger.

You can probably hear it. My voice is calm.
I became very calm.
I feel I'm far away.
Let's say I follow the events
from the shore of a fjord
in Finland or Norway.
It's colder over there.
The heart cools down, too.
It beats more slowly, more peacefully.
Panic attacks avoid me.
I watch the slow flight of a
blackbird feather falling before me.

So I'm thinking
it'd be best to simply burn everything
because I have no strength to put them in order.
Packing the accumulated odd and ends,
selecting what's needed, what's not.
We collected so much unnecessary stuff.
Who has the patience to look it over piece by piece,
then find a good repairman, a painter, a plumber?
(Well, it's almost funny, this unpoetic, recurring
metaphorical idea that the boiler isn't working.
It's amusing, though, that we get
the lowest gas bill ever.

Since the pilot light doesn't work,
we bathe in cold water,
as if in a creek.
Lucky that summer is here.)

I hardly want to go out to the garden.
The last time I found ten strawberries from a plant,
trimmed the white rose,
and planted two tomato settings in a pot.
Then I become tired,
because there isn't an inch of space
that doesn't need some care—
trimming, cutting, and scraping dirt from the tools.
Who can handle all this? Ah, who has the strength,
the faith? How one can live like this?
Or I buy a blue candle, a wine-colored petunia,
a bunch of parsley, a box of blueberries.
The scattered crumbs of faith,
scented, colored signs,
showing that—it seems—
one can live on morsels,
or scratch along among
sooty walls and ruins.
As if in a burnt-out city
after a siege or a fire.

Subdued ≈ Szelidülés

Don't come closer.
Don't leave either.
Don't look at me.
Don't talk.
Sit quietly.
In silence.
I'm covered with wounds.
The lights burn me.
Stay, stay, nevertheless.
But behind the line.
I'm enlightened.
You may wait for me.
Only with closed eyes.
As if you weren't here.

Looming ≈ Átdereng

Last night it was a crow again,
flapping between my ribs.
 It was swaggering
until I woke up from
the wild flapping.
Then it went free.
Before it left
in a desperate rage
it cut my leg
with its beak,
attacking from behind.
The mark, a purple spot, I still wear.
I needed A few days to think and wait for.
the aching purple to dissolve and
green slowly loom over it.

Stare at the Cloud ≈ Bámuld a felhőt

It's been more than two thousand years
Since someone died for me.
That was his last argument.
Still, I don't get it.

𝄢

(This isn't a poem.
It's a Scream, Scream, Scream,
which now is a murderous trap.
Once to scream was his foremost impulse—
collapsed like laid-
out playing cards.
His foundations swayed.
The moth consumed his thorax.)

I should leave, should die.
But quick, but quick, but quick.
Fear nothing and jump into the Danube.
Stab with a knife. Don't be scared.
Bravely trust that death be swift,
I have had enough. Life is beautiful,
but this knife isn't sharp enough.

Calm down, calm down. It's okay.
Lie down a bit quietly.
Stare at the moon, at the cloud.
Others endured too, becoming adult.

It's been more than two thousand years
since someone died for me.
His dying was his last argument.
Slowly, I might understand.

A Million Stitches ≈ Egymillió öltés
To the Tune of a Persian Rug

Day by day. Precisely.
According to a true pattern.
Stitching again and again,
excluding every other motion.
A million stitches. Ultimately, it's infinite.
Proceeding smoothly, turning at the edges,
stitching again and again,
stitching from dawn to dusk.
those who serve
forget their own names.
The pattern is what they know,
guard, and repeat by heart.
They know it by color, by reverse.
recognize it by a stitch—
a star,
    a flower,
        a stem
            a curlicue,
                a leaf.
Weaving is not for those who err from a motif.
The motif is red, and turquoise,
the motif of the heart and the throat.
Its maker is a bird that
sings the tune that was woven in color.
Silently for a year, every tune
would sound as if it was woven into the rug,
so anyone who'll see it would remember this song.
Then the silent bird

—since every voice
will stumble once—
makes a mistake. A single stitch picks
a different color thread.
Later she goes back to the row.
turquoise and red,
                    a star,
                          a stem,
                                a leaf,
                                      a curlicue.
By the time the motif is finished
The weaver will have dark shadows around her eyes.
Her rocking, rounds hips turn rusty,
her hair changes to silver,
She finishes it handsomely beautifully,
closes the motif with care.

The First Reel ≈ Az Első szalag

I'm Etruscan ≈ Etruszk vagyok

I'm Etruscan.
I've been watching time
like those who lean on their elbows
for ages
On one elbow. The eyes are glassy.
Like the statue's on my mother's sarcophagus.
The hair is well arranged. The hand is smooth on the
pillow.
Smooth face. Without features.
What it's looking at is undecidable,
yet the look is fixed
in the in and out attention
without a mirror.
In vain the optomotrist's device
can't calculate the focus.
It's easily understood
that these eyes
aren't motionless and see
only the past and the future
copied on top of each other.
What a montage!
The pictures of a film reeling too quickly.
The reel can't be deciphered
just like the Etruscan marks
on the twisted canvas strips on the mummy.
The posture is rigid,
can't move because then the Etruscan fails.
Invisible, bitter feature around the chin.

Meanwhile, there is an unshakable buoyancy.
It seems though, the wolves are on the move.
Fighting is out of the question.
There is no place to flee, and it's not worth trying.
It'll be neither fast nor slow, but a transition.
This yesterday had happened before,
this tomorrow also.
Time goes forward, backward. Shamelessly hovering
above us, running away.

The Etruscan is Romulus, founder of Rome.

Second Reel ≈ Második szalag
Poets ≈ Költők

They're incapable.
They place their hearts
before you on a china dish
as if it were an apple.
as if it were picked right now,
sliced,
sprinkled with lemon
so it won't turn rusty.
With a touch of sugar
mixed with cinnamon
it becomes sweet,
pungent, and acrid.
Poets string necklaces
from the seeds.
Wear them.
In the meantime
you are sitting in the garden
in a wicker armchair
Shelling the brown beans.
Tearfully
repeating,
well now
how nice a little snack it was.
Poets are content
to feed you well after
their deaths with their hearts.

Third Reel ≈ **Harmadik szalag**

Red Amulet ≈ **Piros amulett**

Tonight a man kissed me in my dream.
The morning was fast approaching—
my mind was filled with it all day.
One day, with an amulet in my heart.

I was coming and going, doing my things.
(Don't even know if he's married or single.)
The secret was red. It surprised me.
So I smiled and was amused.

I sat on a bench with many others.
I think it was a waiting room.
Returning from a long journey,
he approached me directly.

He leaned over me, wearing a brick-red sweater,
as if arriving and meeting was
business as usual, as if it was an old,
common practice between us.

Yet it's absolutely not like this—
according to my dream he is me.
I come home and wait. I fill up a
a whole bench with myself.

I am he, the man wearing the brick-red sweater.
Without packages, his hands are empty,
the waiting room and his long journey,

his coming, the light kiss, and destiny.
I could talk to my doctor
(but my doctor left town).
He'd be interested in
the dreams I dream nowadays.

Alas, it doesn't matter. It's only a dream.
No morning would cope with the dream.

Still, a red amulet in my heart
surely deserves a poem.

Fourth Reel ≈ Negyedik szalag
Report ≈ Riport

Gentlemen, I'd like to report.
Comrades—Tovarisi—please
pay attention a little.
All I want is a minute.
But really, pay attention.
Forgive my words,
but at school
I was ordered to report in Russian
those who were absent at class
Old reflexes, patterns,
so don't be mad at me
that the words about those who missed class
I almost uttered in Russian.
I would report of absence,
if you have time, please.
I'll make it short.
I promise I'll be quick.
A spy deserves as much.
I'm trying hard to be
an excellent spy.
You know, traditionally the poets are watching.
No one is as accurate as they are.
They notice every little sign, and
nowadays the signs aren't very small.
While walking around,
one can't help but realize that
the villages are empty and half
of the country had disappeared.

So I thought if I report this
perhaps you wouldn't go there
where the birds don't fly now,
but will come back in the spring.
But these are people, you know,
who left their nests long ago,
because the roof and the fences
fell in. I know what the
messenger of bad news deserves.
But gentlemen, forgive me.
Grief overwhelms me.
I must tell you
how many are absent.
I miss their voices.
Their footsteps are not echoing
on the half-empty streets.
Only their grandparents shuffle around.
Gentlemen, this won't be good.
There is going to be trouble if hardly
a soul lives and remains in the country.
What would a spy do
if he were the spy for God
(as another spy, namely
Browning, had said it before?)
He couldn't do anything else
but to talk until his throat can do it,
that the fate of something—let's assume
the country—depends on it.
Well gentlemen, I'd like to say goodbye.
Keep enjoying yourselves.

Only a spy reported about
the country and the world.
I didn't mean to disturb.
Only a poet is mourning.

In Hungary during Communism school classes were taught in
Russian. When the class started, one student had to report to
the teachers in Russian how many students were absent. She
is apologizing for starting it out with the Russian word
tovarisi—comrades. She says she was told to report in Russian.

Fifth Reel ≈ Ötödik szalag

Homecoming ≈ Hazatérés

Dream Film ≈ Álomfilm

We are back home. . . ! Well,
the old home, the apartment,
double door angels,
the large, yellow shutters
open to embrace.
The French windows bathing in light—
their gorgeous, slender window boards
sparkle in gold, greet me by
reflecting me. The brass door handles
wave a "we knew it!" They knew
that I could be back!
Back, back! And on and on...!
Other rooms
open up. Old furniture.
Photo albums lie
 in the bottom of drawers.
My God. Ah, my God!
And the homespun fabric and chinaware. . . .
Where do I know this from, where?
Home, home, my home...!
How come I'm seeing you again?

Stay ≈ Maradjon

Memory Film ≈ Emlékfilm

Where
and when?
We are up early,
a grouchy morning
(she who wakes up early,
wakes with worry.)
I don't want cocoa.
Dad is getting dressed. (Is dad good?)
I'm peevish (it seems something has ended)
in the dark, gray, sullen darkness.
(Where is this blurry little room?)
Oops! Waving into the room
because
dad's legs in socks
emerge over the table.
I smile suddenly.
Finally
let it stay that way.
Let it be infinite.

Sixth Reel ≈ Hatodik szalag
White Spot ≈ Fehér folt

I liked to play music.
Mathematics disturbed me.
At the end poetry became
the shore, the lighthouse
where I swam among the waves
and drifting particles.
I swam, swam.
No, not like a shipwrecked woman.
Just like—who knows?—
a particle, or waves,
lights that approach me.
Does anyone know? No, that's not true like this.
Well, like what waves towards and with her
A schoolgirl knows as much,
that this is its nature.
No more, no less.
A simple dot
you wouldn't notice while it moves.
But it was getting dark
—the invisible can be captured
when that dot reached the shore
on the surfer photo.

See, I shot it.
Can you see the white spot on the picture?

Seventh Reel ≈ Hetedik szalag

Laurel Shrubs ≈ Babérbokrok

I wouldn't sell the laurel of friendship
for a sackful of beans.

This deep scent of spice
Flooded the sunny slope
by the thin branches of trees
that were girls before.
Their trunks are firm. But how many people
yearn for their stimulating branches.
since we all used to be Daphnes?
Men are exceptions though.
Foods spiced with laurel
comfort them.
For those whose empty stomachs growl,
bean goulash gives the essence of flavor.
Elyzium for the tired ones.
Leaves rustling and unbound.

Eight Reel ≈ Nyolcadik szalag

Leaf Litter ≈ Avar

Autumn
became long and unexpectedly mild.
Today I went to the garden, the garden
which gave me so much. But I won't stop here.
I trimmed and raked so when winter
arrives it will find the garden in order.
I've found four red tomatoes that ripened a touch late,
and a quince.
A fistful of tiny acorns under the oak wood—
they're the first crop of this tree,
the first tree we've planted here.
I swept too, for the wind blew a bunch of
yellow and brown leaves to the corner and under
the table slats in the patio. I knelt down,
leaned over, rummaging.
The linden trees were rustling,
the oaks were swishing.
I stared at the angular, heart-shaped leaves
gathered on the blue spade.
I turned back to the garden
where the two trees stand.
Their branches aren't touching,
but in autumn they drift together.
Among the fallen leaves,
rest the tips of bushes.
I don't know how the rootlets crawl
towards each other
under the ground.

Ninth Reel ≈ Kilencedik szalag

Private Wound ≈ Saját seb

Psalm of Mary's ≈ Máriák zsoltára

Lord, do not drop sulphur rain and
burning embers on the sinners!
Do not send scorching wind on us!
I beg you as much as I can beg you
and I cannot give you anything in return anymore.
I cannot because my body is not mine,
nor is the child you gave me.
For a long time I've felt that my face, my arms,
my fluttering ebony hair were my own.
Mine were the bright teeth, the high-stepping legs.
My womb my own until a man held me.
And even after that I was my own
mostly in embracing.
When I sang my song flew across the valley.
But mostly I was my own when my son
slipped out of my womb
shining the way the sun appears
from behind relaxing water.
Then my strength left me.
My blood was pouring,
the wound throbbing and gaping
between my thighs.
Thus, I understood the secret of the navel,
the secret of secrets, the ancient bond.
The body you gave me, Lord,
has connected to the flow,

fulfilled the law,
because my breast was filled with milk
and I fed the boy.
His arms were like tiny twigs,
my violet-eyed sweet asterisk.
I knew, I knew well that in vain the blood
in vain milk, in vain navel
he shall be the wound, the
never-expiring, true slash, my Lord.
But what I didn't know, because
your wisdom covered my eyes
—since there is appointed time
for greater and greater wounds,
and it's you who appointed that time
—that the days will come,
the days of darkness
when my son's fragile body,
my violet son's,
my tree branch son's
beautiful body, his arms, chest, and oil-clean skin
will be harmed by pain and slashed by agony,
as if sulfur rain, as if burning embers
fell upon him and his soul was scorched
by blistering wind to dry life inside him.
I didn't count his wounds, my Lord.
Your servant is too weak to do that.
But you, who keep account on the strands of his hair,
you know well why you have allowed this to happen.
I have nothing left, only this empty, gaping wound.
His body, my body is yours.
You have the cure.
Heal his wounds.
Heal my wounds, my Lord.

Tenth Reel ≈ Tizedik szalag

Oil Lamp ≈ Mécses

There are tiny flames—hence the *Limes*.
Clay lamps fit on the palms
driving away darkness, wraiths, phantasms.
Don't let the oil running out, girls.

Let us hope darkness won't grow and bite.
In the rear, the black womb of space lays,
the edge of reality wobbles and sways.
Just the Limes, the Limes must stay alright.
Jar of oil for mindfulness.
Still five girls left. Who will not remember?
Who's not afraid to leave at night with a candle?
Who's not pulled by the bed, though sleepless?

Five of ten. Or three. Or two.
Yet, one is plenty. Scared but intrepid.
Candle in her hands. The camp can sleep.
The limes shine. That will do.

Līmes: a Latin term describing the Germanic border defense of
Ancient Rome, marking the borders of the Roman Empire.
Here they are lamps that mark the boundary.

Eleventh Reel ≈ Tizenegyedik szalag
Times of the Regions of Apparences ≈ Idők a jelenések tájékáról

Dark as dreams flowing from a deep gorge,
crimson flames below.
The shades on the cave's wall soaked in fire.

The morning is amazed by the sky.
Ah! What diversity down below?
I'm among Adonis butterflies
—monochrome mantle above the ground.
But there! That's something! What a land!
It is dressed in insatiable color-ecstasy.

Neighing horses, shot out from bows
run on a fresh, green hill.
Their galloping is the ecstasy of born anew.
I wish I could run along.

Hours. Stars spinning—spinning around.
Translucent times.
Can they be measured or are they unmeasurable?
How many years have I been in the world?

Fawn-eyed dear ones.
The charm is enhanced by the dotted skirts
and the freckles around the nose.
Maybe one day I'll be a deer too?

Giants ships set sail. Their horns blow

break the dim, gray morning
in this smoky harbor at dawn.
The oil-green water shall clear.
Let's go! Let's go!
Who wouldn't like to sail?

Sounds of space-blue glass.
Giant ringing bells from heaven.
How empty the chalice of the sky!
It swings-dongs. Time dies away inside.

Twelfth Reel ≈ Tizenkettedik szalag

Grasshopper Lights ≈ Szöcskefények

For Dezső Tandori and for the others

Light-crickets leap off one by one,
drift, jump from here to beyond,
flee the way the soul slips away
from the body in the end, as it would
escape from this finitude. Most of them
 end up in an urn, but
not the crickets who jump to the
black hole, because all, because all are
Garaboncias'—he saw it beforehand,
knew it beforehand,
that nothing could happen to him,
that it will be like this, this is how it must happen
in that space, in the immaterial
infinite dense core-darkness' need to sparkle.
And the cricket lights spin inside
in a golden spiral, zigzagging,
—dots, liquid gems
masses of shapeless shades around them—
they care not about space-time,
since they remain a perpetual shine.

Dezső Tandori (1938 – 2019) was considered as a
leading Hungarian writer, poet and literary translator.

Garaboncias A character in Hungarian mythology. A brilliant
talker, he is a kind of magician and has diabolical powers,
including the ability to cause storms.

Thirteenth Reel ≈ Tizenharmadik szalag

Captains ≈ Kapitányok

I've met the captains
All are gray haired with
weather-beaten faces.
Each had sunk
at least one ship.
They had been through
and disasters.
None of them have
either a crew or ship.
Yet, their gaits,
their voices and nods,
and the way they stare
toward distant shores
hasn't changed at all.

Fourteenth Reel ≈ Tizennegyedik szalag

Birds ≈ Madarak

Crows ≈ Varjak

Crows are gentle around here
—I can report that.
In the mornings, when the ground is still frozen,
their feet click-clack on the pavement.
They go back and forth, search the grass
around the sleeping fountain,
then further on, under the trees.
They'll find everything the evening
wind knocked from the trees.
Walnuts mostly, but hazelnuts too.
Flying around, carrying their prey in their beaks
for a while. Then they fly back and crack
them open then with firmly repeated motions,
hit the hard shell to the stone smartly.
Could the nuts be the reason for them being gentle?
They come close,
black, hooded.
Their feathers are smooth.
It would be nice to touch,
but I don't want to scare them.
And nothing of Nietzsche,
nothing of homelessness.
They have a home.

Fifteenth Reel ≈ Tizenötödik szalag

Safe Spaces ≈ Biztonságos terek

𝄢

My girlfriend is thinking of
English man in a beige suit.
He's as loyal as *a komondor*
but quieter. He rarely speaks,
but what he says is true.
It's a big deal when he offers his arm,
when we step out of the house
to take a walk or have a meal somewhere.
The color beige is not important,
the important beige outside, inside.
Mixed with milk, coffee, cinnamon, and chocolate.
The infinity, the light, the wind.
So it's the desert.
Isn't it boring? Only for those who never stay
anywhere.

𝄢

I showed a house in the south to my girlfriend.
It's about two thousand kilometers from here,
but it's well light and the garden is divine.
Stone ledges, azulejos,
hibiscus trees, orange grove.
The house looks familiar from the inside.

Just like the interiors at home.
Wouldn't you be alone? Yes.
There it's almost like over here.
I just don't know anyone.

Hungarian sheepdog

Sixteenth Reel ≈ Tizenhatodik szalag
Cunning War ≈   Ravasz háború

It was a long time ago when war raged here.
With declaration of war, armies in uniforms,
with visible heraldries.

Id est broke out already.

The most cunning war
since the beginning of time.
Disguised as peace,
impeccable and unlimited.
There's no shooting,
no visible trenches
or bastions.
The sirens signaling air strikes
are silent.
No one knows when to
take cover,
where the shelters are.

Still, there are shootings.
They're bombing the mind,
place mines in the fields of silence.
The brain splits in two without bloodshed.
Thoughts torn to shreds
circulate in the skulls.
But blood's flowing, too.
Wounds inflicted with blades
on thin arms and tight,

young thighs of teenagers.
They pierce their tongues,
draw needle marks on their skin
because a mark is needed.
Our bodies demand a mark,
to leave a mark,
to reveal the hidden war.
And they starve as well,
if they want to.
Until death.
Though, there is no siege,
no living in a basement.
They grow prisoner-thin next to
packed full refrigerators
and with eyes widened in horror
they watch accusingly
what is going on.
Yet they can't avoid the cunning trap.

They reject the attributes of peace.
—bouillon, crepes, œufs à la neige—
with disgust.
We don't want, don't want, don't want
the cunning and evil peace,
the beguiling warmth of the kitchen.
Nobody escapes
who doesn't take cover.
Ah, snail shell,
ah, shelter,
ah, where to hide
to finish it?

Seventeenth Reel ≈ **Tizenhetedik szalag**

Leaven in Three Measures of Flour ≈
Kovász három mérőnyi lisztben

In the Spring of two thousand twenty
—in a time rushing through a spiral of fog—
fear crawled upon the bastion wall of
ordinary days. Fasting came in its wake.

Though there's a new nest in a linden tree hollow,
redeeming buds on the bushes,
the crocuses are all ready for the holiday—
but mankind—my Lord, don't get me wrong—
is in trouble. What now happens to Earth, to us,
—a code, the virus, risk for disease,
the hideous crown of the prim-ordeal evil, there's
no chance to foresee mankind's dark gimmicks.

So, my Lord, now mankind is far away from you
and the Father and Son.
We don't touch even each other, especially
Those who have a cold. No hugs, no one dares to kiss.
Every soul hides in masks, in gloves.
Planetary mice in an experiment. That's what we
became, my Lord. Creatures. Our faces turning
gray, and narrowing our space to stay.

And this insolent virus is mimicking you
—never had so many crowns of thorns!—
but without your presence, ah, where else
you could find that thing if not before your eyes.

Be the leaven!
Heaven in three measures of flour,
when the feast of the unleavened bread
shines upon us
where we'd be with you on Mount Olive
(ah, don't let the sky, our faces, be gray!)
Thirsty for solace and hope,
let us know you're coming for us and we'll go to you!)
in two thousand twenty, in the time of Lent.

THE POETS

Borbála Kulin (1979, Budapest) literary critic, editor, poet. Graduated at Eötvös Loránd University with a degree in Latin Language and Literature and Hungarian Language and Literature. Finished her PhD in 2015 at the University of Debrecen as literary critic. She lived in the United States, Virginia between 2012 and 2014. Editor in chief of „A Vörös Postakocsi" literary magazine since 2009. She has been publishing poems, translations and short novels since 2013. Currently lives in Debrecen. Her books: The Edited Correspondence of Gyula Illyés and Ladislas Gara (2007); Ethics and Aesthetics in the Oeuvre of Gyula Illyés (2018), I Just Love (poems, forthcoming). Awards: The Award of Hungarian Fiction Writers in category of lyrics, János Arany Memorial Year, 2018.

Zita Izsó was born in Budapest in 1986. Her first poetry collection, Tengerlakó (Sea Dweller), won the Gérecz Attila Prize for the Year's Best Debut Novel in 2012. With her first drama, which she wrote with her sister, she won the Hungarian Radio Playwriting Contest. The Debrecen Színláz Company took her second drama entitled Függés (Dependence) to the stage in 2010. Her second poetry collection, Színről színre (Face to Face), was published in 2014. Since 2015, she and the Hungarian photographer Máté Bach have run The Pest Woman blog. In 2017, they published a book of collected interviews from the blog under the same title. Zita's poems have been translated into English, German, Arabic, Turkish, Czech, Polish, Serbian, Slovak, Romanian and Bulgarian. She published her third poetry collection in 2018 under the title Éjszakai földet érés (Nighttime Landing). She is one of the editors of theFISZ-Kalligram Horizons World Literature Series, the 1749.hu – World Literature Magazine, the Pannon Tükör literature review and the Üveghegy Children's Literature website. She translates English, German, French, and Spanish writers, including the Argentinian poet Alejandra Pizarnik and the Mexican poet Rosario Castellanos. She is the recipient of numerous awards and grants, including the Móricz Zsigmond Literary Grant, the Babits Mihály Literary Translator Grant, and the NKA Arts Grant.

Krisztina Rita Molnar poet, writer, literary translator born in Budapest, 1967. She is the author of 15 books. She has 4 books of original poetry (Közelkép {Close-up} , Littera Nova Publisher, 1998.; Különlét {Being my Other}, PONT Publisher, 2008.; Kőház {Stone House}, Scolar Publisher, 2013.; Levél egy fjord partjáról (Letter from the shore of a fjord), Scolar 2017), 1 book of short stories (Remélem, örülsz {I hope, you are glad}, Scolar, 2019), 8 novels for children, one of which is the famous Maléna kertje {Malena's Garden}, Naphegy Publisher, 2013.), A book on creative writing and one book of translation of Zen Shorts by Jon J Muth. She is a high school teacher of Hungarian grammar and literature, but for five years she has been a free-lance writer and teacher of creative writing. She is a member of the Society of Hungarian Authors and the Hungarian Literary Translators' Association. Her important prizes are the Salvatore Quasimodo special prize for poetry in 2009, Nizzai kavics-díj 2010 {Pebble of Nice-prize}; Spangár András-díj 2011 {a prize for the best short story}; Szépíró-díj 2018 {the prize from the Society of Hungarian Authors for the best authors}; Bárka-díj 2020 {the prize from the Bárka Literary and Art Magazine} In 2019 she got the writer's scholarship of Visegrad Fund to Krakow for a quarter of a year. Her new poetry volume titled Linenbook will be published in the spring of next year.

TRANSLATOR

Gabor G Gyukics (b. 1958) poet, jazz poet, literary translator born in Budapest. He is the author of 11 books of original poetry, 6 in Hungarian, 2 in English, 1 in Arabic, 1 in Bulgarian, 1 in Czech, 1 book of original prose, and 17 books of translations including *A Transparent Lion*, selected poetry of Attila József and *They'll Be Good for Seed, a Contemporary Hungarian Poetry* (in English, both with co-translator Michael Castro) and an anthology of North American Indigenous poets in Hungarian entitled *Medvefelhő a város felett*. He writes his poems in English (his second language) and Hungarian. He lived in Holland for two years before moving to the US where he'd lived between 1988-2002. At present he resides in Szeged, Hungary. His latest book in English entitled *a hermit has no plural* was published by Singing Bone Press in 2015. His latest book in Hungarian was published by Lector Press in 2018. In 2020, he received the Hungary Beat Poet Laureate Lifetime award by the National Beat Poetry Foundation Inc. USA. He is a recipient of the Banff International Literary Translation Centre (BILTC) residency in Canada in 2011.

COVER ART

Sára Pozsgai was born in 1986 in Berettyóújfalu, Hungary. She moved to the Netherlands in December 2009 where she started painting in 2015. Her paintings are characterized by surreal, figurative, and abstract

images and strong use of color. She had several group
and solo exhibitions in Hungary and elsewhere.

PREFACE

Dr. Orsolya Rakai is a literary scholar and
Associate Professor of the University of Szeged

www.ingramcontent.com/pod-product-compliance
Lightning Source LLC
LaVergne TN
LVHW021507080426
835509LV00018B/2431